ISBN: 149936041X
ISBN-13: 978-1499360417

CONTENTS

I-Establish Goals   Pg.1

1. Define Winning

II-Clear Your Head   Pg. 3

2. Keep Your Emotions Out of It

3. Don't Use it to Get Even With the Other Side

4. Get the Facts Before You Make a Decision

5. Listening to Lawyers, Not Other People

III-Preparing for Divorce   Pg. 11

6. Involve Your Friends and Family

7. The Benefits of Therapy

8. Support Groups

9. Is There Any Benefit to Waiting?

10. Life is Short

IV-Selecting a Lawyer   Pg. 17

11. You Need a Lawyer for Every Case

12. Cost

13. Billing Practices

14. Retainer Agreement

15. Is Your Lawyer Looking Out for You or Someone Else?

16. Communication

17. What Matters and What Doesn't

V-Developing a Battle Plan   **Pg. 23**

18. Know the Process

19. Know the Law

20. Stay Off the Internet

21. Ask Questions

22. You're the Boss

23. Getting From Point A to Point B

24. Welcome to Your New Job (Start Now)

25. What is Your Realistic Budget?

VI-Mediation and Other ADR Options   **Pg. 29**

26. Find Out What is Available in Your Area

27. Mediation as an Alternative

28. Mediation as Part of the Divorce Case

29. Arbitration

30. Negotiation

VII-Negotiation Strategy   **Pg. 33**

31. Timing is Everything

32. Negotiations With Your Spouse

33. Get All the Facts Before Starting

34. Using Negotiation Statements

VIII-Settlement Strategy   **Pg. 37**

35. Facts vs. Emotion

36. Fighting Solves Nothing

37. Does Your Lawyer Tell You No?

38. Move Around Logjams

IX-Alimony Issues   **Pg. 41**

39. Money is Money

40. Understand Tax Implications

41. Discuss All What If Scenarios

42. Lump Sum vs. Period Payments

43. Imputation of Income

X-Child Support   **Pg. 45**

44. Know the Rules

45. Have the Numbers

46. What and When Will This Change?

47. What Does it Cover?

48. Child Support May be Used as Alimony

49. When Does it End?

50. What About College?

XI-The Marital Residence   **Pg. 49**

51. Don't Get Attached to It

52. Use a Good Real Estate Agent

53. Scrutinize Appraisal

XI-Personal Property   **Pg. 53**

54. Don't Get Your Lawyer Involved

55. Deal With This Before Divorce is Over

XIII-Child Custody   **Pg. 55**

56. Know the Law

57. Consider Practical Reality

58. Put Everything in Writing

59. Using Parenting Coordinators

60. Change in Circumstances

61. When Can Children Make Their Own Decision?

62. Dealing With Parental Alienation

XIV-Litigating Financial Issues   **Pg. 61**

63. Closely Held Business

64. Dealing With Under the Table Income

65. Using Forensic Accountants

66. Discovery Tools

67. Look at Your Post-Divorce Life

XV-Litigating Child Custody Issues   **Pg. 67**

68. Mentally Prepare For War

69. Consider Post-Divorce Life

70. Keep a Journal

71. Line up Your Witnesses

72. What's on the Internet?

73. Gathering Additional Evidence?

74. Using Experts

75. Throwing Mud

76. Deflecting Mud Thrown at You (Deal With it Early)

XVI-Trial   **Pg. 73**

77. Limit the Issues

78. Using Stipulations

79. Do You Have a Strategy?

80. Is Your Lawyer Organized?

81. Settlement Discussions During Trial

82. Relax

83. Time Frame and Cost of Trial

84. Appeal Process

85. Standard of Review / Odds

86. Time Frame and Cost of Appeal

XVII-Drafting the Settlement   Pg. 81

87. Must be Comprehensive

88. Include the Why

89. Examine All What If Scenarios

90. Read it Carefully at Least 10 Times (Have Others Read it)

91. Ask Many Questions

92. Vacating a Settlement Agreement

XVIII-Post Divorce Motions   Pg. 85

93. Modifying Support Obligation

94. Modifying Custody

95. Talk to Your Lawyer About When to Act

XIX-Post Divorce Life   Pg. 89

96. Keep a Journal

97. Save Money For Legal Fees

98. Don't Sweat the Small Stuff

99. Post-Divorce Counseling

100. Don't Involve Children

101. Don't Give up the Fight

ACKNOWLEDGMENTS

Thanks as always to all of my clients and employees. Special thanks to Bonnie Jeanne Horwath who helped me edit this book.

I. ESTABLISH GOALS

1. Define Winning

How will you know that you have won unless you establish from the beginning what winning will really look like? Since you are not a lawyer, you may not be able to fully appreciate all of the issues that will arise during your case. Thus, I don't expect you to plan out an exact settlement of your case. Instead, you should be able to think about the end of your case in general terms.

-Do you want custody of the children or just a good parenting time schedule?

-Are you seeking alimony?

-Do you want to keep the house?

-Do you want to have a good relationship with your ex?

-Do you want to avoid spending a ton of money on legal fees?

   Or are your interests different?

-Do you want to bury your ex?

-Do you want to leave him or her with nothing?

Whatever you decide, you should have some idea as to what you are trying to achieve. Keep in mind that your goals may change over time. Victory today may seem different than victory tomorrow. That is quite all right. People change, as does life. However, you need some type of plan going into your case so that you can guide yourself and your lawyer. Otherwise, you will be approaching the entire case in a haphazard fashion without any sense as to where you are trying to go. When you do get to the end of the case, you may feel dissatisfied; not because the outcome wasn't the best for you, but because you never really had an idea as to what you were trying to achieve.

Another way to view it is . . . if you don't know where you are going, how are you going to know when you get there?

I have seen too many people spend all of their time and money fighting in court even years after the divorce case is over. They weren't happy with the end of the case, and they may never be happy no matter what happens. I think many of these people never defined victory. As a result, their lives have become an endless fight over nothing. Don't become one of these people. Define winning now so you'll know what it looks like when you get there. Just remember, winning is rarely getting just a little more than the other side.

II. CLEAR YOUR HEAD

2. Keep Your Emotions Out of It

If you read through #2 and never get to #3, you will still walk away with a great amount of advice from this book. I cannot stress enough that you have to take your emotions out of your divorce case. I'll repeat that. **Take your emotions out of your divorce case.** To which most people will reply, *but I can't*! Nonsense! You can do anything, you just have to try. Will you always succeed? Probably not, but you have to try.

Of course, you are hiring an attorney because he or she should be able to take the emotions out of the case. They (should) act more or less as a filter. However, your attorney cannot make the decisions for you. In the end, you have to make the final call (see #22). If you don't work on taking the emotional issues out of the case, you will spend more money and make senseless decisions. I have seen it time and time again. Remember, I'm not simply making this stuff up. I am using my experience to help you.

In business, when people are negotiating a settlement, a contract, or anything else, they take the emotion out of it. It becomes a matter of dollars and cents; basically risk analysis. They ask what the pros and cons are and weigh the options in the case, contract, etc. What is in the company's best interests? This is how you must approach your divorce case.

I always tell my clients that getting divorced is a lot like winding down a business. The business has assets and liabilities that must be dealt with just like the marriage does. Of course, there are some extra issues such as children and support, but in business there may also be employees and other compensation issues. The biggest difference with divorce is that the two parties in the case were once in love with each other and now they are not. However, that has nothing to do with how the case will be resolved. The law is emotionless you must be too.

When you get emotional about any aspect of your case, your reaction is based on that emotion and not logic. Emotional decisions are often rash and not in your best interest. More importantly, they can lead to stress which could cause a number of health issues including, but limited to heart problems. It can also lead to over use of prescription drugs or self-medication via drugs and alcohol; all of which can lead to serious problems for your case. I've seen clients who were in the best of health in the beginning of their case suddenly suffer heart attacks in the middle of it due to stress, some of them fatal. I've seen others abuse substances and lose custody or parenting time as a result.

Being too emotional can also cost you a great deal of money. Unfortunately, many lawyers may not talk you out of making senseless moves in your case. Instead, some will actually fan the flames of your emotion and convince you to *bury your spouse* or to otherwise take a scorched earth approach to get even. The only person who is going to benefit here is your lawyer and most likely your spouse's lawyer. At some point, you will probably come to your senses and realize that you were taken advantage of, or *screwed over*. Regardless, I don't think you will ever really be satisfied by screwing over your spouse.

No one said this was going to be easy. I'm sure you'll never meet anyone that will tell you that divorce is fun, and I realize that taking the emotion out of it will not be easy, but you need to focus on your victory and work hard at letting it all go. You may have to make some profound life changes to find a way to deal with the stress and loss that comes with divorce. Perhaps therapy, religion, a new hobby, exercise, counseling, or something else will help you deal with everything on your plate. Maybe it's a combination of things. If you don't try, you'll never succeed. Try looking into a support group or creating one of your own.

One thing you should not do is to turn to medication, drugs, or alcohol to relive your stress. I have nothing against prescription medication; millions of functioning adults take something or another to keep them in balance. However, resorting to prescription medication during a divorce could cause serious problems. Speak to your lawyer first if you are on medication for mental health issues such as anxiety and/or depression or if you are thinking about it. You don't want to take any action that could impact your case. The same goes for any type of therapy. Make sure that this cannot be turned around and used against you.

Because this is the most important part of this book, I want to give you a prime example of how emotion can impact you. In this case, I represented the wife in New Jersey. Her husband had filed for divorce but she didn't pick up the papers until she hired me. She brought them right to my office and we read them together. She flat out lost it due to all of the allegations about her involving drug use, alcoholism, etc.

In New Jersey, the divorce complaint is rather meaningless. Gone are the days of having to make allegations against your spouse, you only need to say that you want to get divorced, the reason why is basically irrelevant. Nevertheless, in this case, one of the causes of action for divorce was extreme mental cruelty which is where the other attorney included all of these allegations against my client. It went on for several pages.

Looking at this from a strategic perspective, this was a dumb move by the other side. There was no reason to include any of those allegations. It would not give the husband any sort of advantage in the case, nor would anyone look at it and take the children away from my client. So all the husband really accomplished was to make himself feel better by throwing some mud at his wife. Clearly it took some time for his attorney to get all of this information, type it up, have the client review it, make edits, finalize it, etc. All of this extra time could have resulted in an extra $300 to $800 worth of attorney fees. For what? Absolutely nothing. The husband was approaching this case from an emotional perspective and his attorney took advantage of him.

If money is not really an object to you, look at it this way. Instead of building up a case in secret, this attorney put his cards on the table. This allowed me to gather all my troops quickly and thoroughly. I calmed my client down and we can up with a plan. We put together substance abuse evaluations, psychological evaluations and over a dozen character letters. By the time any of this reached court (by way of a motion the other attorney filed a few weeks later), we were well prepared to answer everything. Had the husband filed a normal divorce complaint and otherwise kept quiet about these allegations until the right time, I would have had to rush to slap something together in a short amount of time.

My client in this case was not perfect however. One of the reasons the husband even made any of these allegations against her was because she was on anti-anxiety medication as a result of the deterioration of the marriage shortly before the divorce was filed. She also drank on at least one occasion where the police were called. While she was not caring for the children at that time, that incidence gave some credibility to the rest of the husband's claims about her alleged alcoholism.

As I said before, when my client received the divorce complaint she flipped out. She was screaming and yelling about all of the allegations contained in the complaint, even though I explained to her that none of it mattered and it would actually help us, as I previously related. Likewise, whenever a letter came over from the other attorney, she would get upset even though none of the allegations mattered. It was not as if we were in front of the judge; it was merely words on paper but she, like many other clients, would almost lose it.

Luckily for my divorce client, I eventually taught her how to take the emotional issues out of the case. Trust me when I tell you that it wasn't easy. It must have taken at least two dozen conversations over a month long period. It also wasn't perfect. I had to remind her quite often to calm down. The good news is that she listened to me. She recognized when she was being emotional and we developed strategies to discuss issues without emotion. For example, if we got something from the other side that was upsetting, I advised her to read it, put it down, distract herself with something else and then come back to it a day or so later. This way, the initial sting is removed and any decision made is not under the gun or in the heat of passion.

Another example of the danger of emotions comes from a child abuse case. I had a client who was a recovering drug addict being accused of using drugs again. She was dealing with the child protection agency on her own. She got so upset that someone accused her of using drugs again after she had been clean for so long that she actually fell off the wagon and started using again. Only at that point did she call me. Had she thought more clearly from day one, she would have called me earlier and let me take care of everything.

Again, if you take nothing else away from this book except this point, I will have done my job. You will likely save a lot of money and get a better result. You will also be healthier and happier. If that isn't winning, I don't know what is.

3. Don't Use Your Divorce to Get Even With the Other Side

If you have defined winning properly and you have taken the emotion out of the case, you should not be looking to 'get even'. In most divorce cases, the reason for the divorce is irrelevant. As I often tell my clients, if the other side is the best person in the world or the worst person in the world, they still get half the house. Unless they are a danger to the children, they are going to see them or even have a shot at getting custody. A divorce is not an opportunity to get back at or get even with your spouse. Attempting to use it as such will waste your time and money and may even backfire on you.

Even if you live in a state where the reason for getting divorced may have some type of impact on the outcome of an issue, make sure that your actions are motivated by strategy and not revenge.

4. Get the Facts Before You Make a Decision

Continuing with our theme of taking the emotion out of the case, you need facts to make a decision. Judges apply the law to the facts and you should as well. If you are presented with a settlement or any other decision, understand the facts at play.

-What will happen if you say yes and what will happen if you say no?

-Are there other options?

-Are there risks?

-Is this in your benefit?

If you don't have the facts, you are basing your decision on either assumption or emotion. Either way, you are probably making the wrong decision. Regardless, you are certainly not making an informed decision.

5. Listen to Lawyers, Not Other People

When you are going through a divorce, it seems like everyone around you turns into an amateur lawyer. They know everything because they went through one case. Or maybe they know a guy that knows a guy. You wouldn't accept medical advice from a plumber just as you won't ask a doctor how to unclog your drain. Thus, don't accept legal advice from anyone except a lawyer.

This is especially true for family members. In some cultures, each spouse won't do anything without asking a number of family members. This is why I say that at times it's as if entire families are getting divorced. Every lawyer has probably been there. In some cases, we rarely speak to the client but instead, we get calls from numerous relatives. Also, instead of just meeting with our client, our office is filled with almost a dozen people all with different opinions and questions.

If anyone other than a lawyer tells you anything about your divorce case or the divorce process in general, take it with a giant mountain of salt. Feel free to run it by your divorce lawyer but do not act upon it. I can tell you that 90% of the time, the advice or information that my client has been given by non-lawyers is wrong. In fact, some of it can be very damaging. When in doubt, call a lawyer and then trust in that lawyer's advice.

III. PREPARING FOR DIVORCE

6. Involve Your Friends and Family

I realize that I just told you not to rely on what other people tell you and now I am telling you to talk to your friends and family. There is a difference. Divorce is not easy. In fact, it could be the most difficult thing you ever do. Everything about your life may change and it can be quite scary. You shouldn't go at it alone and your lawyer is not a therapist. Thus, you should use your friends and family as a support system.

Hopefully your support system is there to support you and not tell you what to do. They can give you feedback and maybe share their experiences but in the end, they shouldn't try to control your decision making. You have to understand that every case, no matter how similar, is different. What your friends or family members got may be different then what you get.

Too many people are scared of what others may think of them especially if some dirty laundry gets aired out. We have all made mistakes. If your friends and family truly care for you, they accept you no matter what has happened. If not, they are probably not a true friend. Furthermore, using a support system can help you remain grounded so you can make better decisions.

7. The Benefits of Therapy

I'm not against therapy nor do I think that everyone needs it for every little thing. Instead, it is an option that should at least be considered. As I previously indicated, you should discuss this with your lawyer to make sure that this will not come back to bite you in the divorce case. You could place your mental health at issue whereas it wouldn't otherwise be a problem.

There are many benefits of therapy and one of the biggest ones is that it gives you an opportunity to 'check in'. You are approaching this case or any other issue from a certain view point. Having a neutral person, especially one with training and experience to talk with can be a huge value. Maybe after a couple sessions your therapist will decide that you don't need therapy and that you are fine. It's nice to know that a professional feels that you are on the right path. Maybe he or she will have some advice or other options that you never thought of.

If therapy will not impact your divorce case, then it does not carry any risk. At that point, there is simply no reason not to give it a shot. It could help you make a proper decision so that you don't regret making the wrong one later.

8. Support Groups

Support groups should also be considered. Like some of these other options, it might not be right for everyone. However, there is a certain comfort by just knowing that other people are going through the exact same situation or that others have done it and survived it. You may have a lot of questions about the process and your post-divorce life that your lawyer cannot answer. The people you meet at the support group may be able to answer your questions and help guide you along the way. Others may offer ideas or new perspectives on various issues regarding your case.

By at least considering this option, you will know that your decision to file was made with as much input as possible.

9. Is There any Benefit to Waiting?

Developing an ostrich mentality solves nothing. I am always amazed by the people that know that their marriage is over and yet wait to file for divorce. Fear of the unknown is likely the culprit here and most have not followed points #6, #7, and #8. Instead, they kick the can down the road hoping that it will somehow resolve itself one day. Of course, that's probably never going to happen.

More importantly, there could be serious legal consequences to waiting. For example, if you were to get divorced now, you may have to pay one amount to your spouse. If you wait a few years, this amount could triple because of a number of issues including but not limited to a change in fact (i.e. one spouse becomes disabled), the law (after a certain amount of years, something becomes automatic), you make a certain move that has serious but unforeseen ramification or there is a change in the law.

Here is an example from a big case I had. A client had money in an account from an inheritance. For reasons known only to him, he added his wife's name to that account. Shortly after, he hired an attorney to file for divorce. However, he held off for about a year until he filed for good. As a result, he now co-mingled those funds and was at risk of having to give his wife half. Had he filed when he originally wanted to, he could have argued that he filed so soon after doing this that the co-mingling has little to no effect. By all accounts, that would have been a very successful argument. While I worked out an amazing settlement for him, he still paid tens of thousands more than he would have had he stuck with his original filing date.

I know what you are thinking: but what if I am not sure or change my mind. Again, this is where you need to speak to a lawyer. Just because you file for divorce, doesn't mean you will get divorced. About 5% of divorce cases end in reconciliation. Furthermore, the filing date of the divorce may carry significant consequences. Thus, if you aren't 100% sure, talk to your lawyer about filing for divorce while you explore the idea of staying married.

If you do call off the divorce case, it should probably be pretty simple. At that point, your lawyer may be able to draft some type of an agreement that governs at least some of the issues between you. This is sometimes referred to as a mid-marriage agreement. Using the example I gave above, the client could have reached a mid-marriage agreement with his wife. Such an agreement could have made it clear that the wife's name is on the account for convenience purposes only and that absent adding marital funds into the account, she would have no claim to any of the funds in the account in the event of a divorce.

10. Life is Short

We all know the saying *life is short* but how many people really put this saying to use? I speak to way too many clients who have told me how miserable they have been for the latter part of the marriage or for others almost the entire marriage. Why keep this up? No matter how long you live, you only have so many years on this planet. Why spend any of this in chaos and misery?

Yes your post-divorce life may be scary and it may be lonely at times. However, anything is probably better than the hell you have been living through. Instead of focusing on the negative aspects of the divorce, use it as a positive. Change your life for the better. Become a better friend or a better parent. Try new things, go new places, meet new people. Now I'm not trying to kick-start a midlife crisis here, so don't blow all your money on an expensive sports car. Instead, embrace the opportunity you have to improve your life or even re-boot it. Not a lot of people have that opportunity.

Only you can create your own happiness but if you are living in misery in a marriage that has been over for a long time, you will be stuck in a rut wasting your life away. What if you only had a few years left to live? Is this how you would like to spend it?

IV. SELECTING A LAWYER

11. You Need a Lawyer for Every Case

No one in their right mind would attempt to perform surgery on themselves. However, there are some people that think they can avoid having to pay for a lawyer by doing the divorce themselves. They purchase a *divorce kit* from somewhere, go to mediation, or otherwise just wing it. Handling any legal matter without a lawyer is just insane. Look at it this way, lawyers hire other lawyers, so why shouldn't you? I have hired several lawyers for various matters. Could I have handled those matters by myself? Probably, but I'm not willing to roll the dice and neither should you.

Sure there are some people that represent themselves and turn out okay. However, there are also plenty of other people where the case blows up in their face. In that case, those people find that it can be very expensive to hire a lawyer to clean up your mess; possibly three times more than what the divorce itself would have cost you. Thus, don't take this gamble. Find a good lawyer and hire him or her.

12. Cost

As the old saying goes, you get what you pay for. Don't be penny-wise and pound foolish. However, you want the cost to be in proportion to what you are fighting over. For example, if you don't have kids and there are no assets, it shouldn't cost you $10,000 to get divorced. However, if you are going to war over the children, have a number of assets and/or liabilities and a possibly alimony obligation, you should be prepared to pay accordingly.

It helps to always keep the big picture in mind. For example, a client called me up to inquire about mediation. Although he makes six figures, he really wants to save money. While I am a big fan of mediation, I explained that I don't think saving money on legal fees should be his goal here. He is looking at paying permanent alimony and a lot of it. If he pays an additional $10,000 per year because he went through mediation, that's $200,000 over 20 years. Paying a $5,000 extra up front for a lawyer to save $200,000 over 20 years sounds good right? He never thought about that and he liked this approach better. Of course, I've had mediation clients who were fine with giving up over a million dollars that they were entitled to. Everyone has their own sets of goals and values and the theme of this book is to determine your own and work towards them.

13. Billing Practices

While you don't want to be cheap, you don't want to be ripped off either. Most lawyers will charge you an upfront retainer fee and charge by the hour. This retainer fee is a credit that you have with the office. In other words, you are prepaying for the time that may be spent on the case. The lawyer will then provide you with an invoice from time to time to show you how much of your retainer is used, and bill accordingly if need be. Review this invoice carefully and make sure that your lawyer isn't playing any games. Don't be afraid to ask questions.

I had one lawyer fax a letter to my office even though the court already did. So whenever the court sent me something, I had to get it twice. In essence, the other lawyer is billing twice for the same document (once to read it and again to send me a letter with it). Another thing that I have seen is when a group of lawyers in the same firm get together to conference a case. Conferencing a case is normal since two heads are better than one. However, you shouldn't have to pay for two or even four lawyers to talk about your case as the same time! I've seen people pay a combined hourly rate exceeding $1,000 because four lawyers were discussing their case. This is just a straight rip off.

If your lawyer rips you off, your net settlement will be lessened. Keep in mind that mistakes do happen. If it is just a mistake, ask that it be corrected. If you are getting ripped off, fire that lawyer and hire someone else.

14. Retainer Agreement

This might sound obvious but you need to have a signed contract with your lawyer that explains how much you paid, what you paid for, what your lawyer represents you for and does not represent you for, what the hourly billing rate is, when future payments are due, what costs you will be billed for and at what rate, etc. I've seen lawyers demand money from clients just because they wanted more money. Since some clients can be scared, they actually pay it even though it's not owed. While some jurisdictions require that your retainer is refundable, make sure that the fee agreement says that it is. This way, if you reconcile or change lawyers, you are not going to lose all of your money.

15. Is Your Lawyer Looking Out for You or Someone Else?

In populated areas with a lot of lawyers, you may not have to worry about the good ole boy network. However, in smaller areas, this should be a big concern. What happens is that many divorce lawyers focus most if not all of their time on divorce and in one specific area. As a result, the same small groups of lawyers see each other in court every day and they see each other at various lawyer functions such as bar association meetings and continuing legal education classes. This leads many to develop friendships, some of them so deep that their children hang out together. How then can they put this friendship aside to battle each other over your case? Remember, when your case is long over, they will still have to deal with each other both in and out of the court room.

Due to these relationships, your lawyer may have more of an allegiance to the other lawyer than you. You need someone that can work with the other lawyer and the judge in an aggressive but polite manner. However, you need someone that can wage an all-out war against the other side if that is called for. Thus, when selecting a lawyer, ask them about their relationships with other lawyers. Make sure that they will fight for you above all else.

16. Communication

One of the biggest complaints about lawyers is lack of communication. Lawyers can get very busy and it's easy for a message to get lost in the shuffle. I don't suggest that you fire a lawyer over one communication snafu. However, if you can never reach your lawyer, this is a big problem. When you first meet with your lawyer, ask how you will communicate with him or her. Just remember that your lawyer will be more expensive than a 1-900- number. Thus, don't use him or her as a therapist. Cover what you need to cover and that's it.

Communication is more than just how often you speak with your lawyer or whether or not your lawyer returns your calls. You need to understand exactly what is going on with your case. If you don't, be sure to ask questions. If you don't understand the process, how do you know if you are on the path to winning your case?

17. What Matters and What Doesn't?

The following aspects about your lawyer do not matter at all: age, race, gender, religion, type of car they drive, how their office looks or how close they are to the court house. I love hearing how someone needs a male lawyer or a female lawyer. Or when someone says, I hired him or her because their office was right near the court house. This is just ridiculous.

Some people think that a judge will react differently to a male or female lawyer. I've never seen this and there is simply no logic behind it. Any of those other reasons are even more ludicrous. You need to base your decision on your lawyer's qualifications. Anyone can sign a lease to rent an office near the court house. There are no prequalifications.

What matters is how your lawyer interacts with you and how well he or she will represent you in your case. As previously indicated, this needs to be done without ripping you off. Thus, a lawyer that will fight for you at a reasonable price is your best choice regardless of anything else.

V. DEVELOPING A BATTLE PLAN

18. Know the Process

How will you know if you are on the path to victory if you don't even understand the process? You need to understand how the entire case will unfold. I have written a book explaining the process in New Jersey so my clients don't have to waste their time or money asking me to explain everything in great detail. Of course, if they have questions, I'll answer them. Either way, you need to understand what will happen and when.

19. Know the Law

No matter how much time your lawyer spends with you, it is impossible to give you a law school education in the middle of your case. However, you need to know the basics. You don't need to do this from day one but at some point, you need to know what you are up against. How is child support calculated? How is child custody decided? What about alimony? You need an overview of the law on all of the issues in your case. If you don't understand the law, you won't know what to ask for. Developing a plan to win will be very difficult.

20. Stay Off the Internet

The Internet is a blessing and a curse. It helps clients find lawyers, research them and get a better handle on the law. However, too many people read something on the Internet and then think that they know everything about the law. The last thing a lawyer wants to hear is 'but on the Internet it says . . .'

In the end, you have to trust your lawyer. If you find something on the Internet that is completely contrary to what your lawyer says, then by all means ask him or her about it. Just be sure that you do it in the right way. The problem with the Internet is that people read it, accept it as true and then when told otherwise, they get confrontational. That can really erode the trust you are trying to build with your lawyer.

The Internet is also full of false information, outdated information, information pertaining to other states and information that may not apply to your case. Thus, it's probably best to put it down unless you really know what you are doing and know where to look.

21. Ask Questions

While I don't want you to spend all of your time on the Internet looking up information, I want you to be informed. It's hard for lawyers to remember what it's like to be a normal person. While we do our best to explain the process and the issues to our clients, it's easy to forget that clients may have no idea as to what to expect, what the options are, etc. You should know exactly what is going on with your case and what the plan is even if the plan is to come up with a plan! Do not be afraid to ask questions and no question is a stupid question.

22. You're the Boss

When it comes down to it, you're the boss. You run the show and what you say goes. If you want to trust in your lawyer's advice and go in whatever direction he or she suggests, that's fine. However, it should be your choice to do that instead of them forcing you do something. Trust me, I will lean on my client to do something if I think it is in their best interests but in the end, I won't force them.

If you trust your lawyer and your lawyer explains everything to you, it should be pretty easy. If you and your lawyer disagree that much, it might be time to either seek a second opinion or hire a new lawyer. I often tell my clients that it's my job to explain the options and render advice so they can make the final decision. Even if a client wants to follow my advice without me having to give an explanation, I still explain it so that they understand it.

23. Getting From Point A to Point B (The Battle Plan)

Now that you understand how to clear your mind, find a good lawyer and get the information you need, you need a plan. How will you and your lawyer end this case? In most cases, the lawyer probably can't sit down with you on day one and map out the entire case. That would be like mapping out an entire chess match or football game. It's impossible because you don't know what the other side will do.

The plan to win your case develops over time but there is always a plan. You should at least understand the big picture so that you can make sure your case is moving towards that end result. For simple cases the plan might be to just get the information everyone needs to resolve the case. For more complicated cases, I come up with a battle plan. No matter how cordial the lawyers may be with each other, every case is a battle in one form or another.

That also holds true if your case is going to mediation. Mediation is a form of negotiation and every negotiation needs a strategy. If you don't have a plan for this battle, there is no way you can map out your strategy. As a result, you will proceed in a haphazard manner and your case will be severely impacted as a result.

You shouldn't have to come up with your own battle plan; that's your lawyer's job. However, you need to make sure one actually exists and to understand how the plan will unfold over time.

24. Welcome to Your New Job (Start Now)

As part of the battle plan, you will be given a number of assignments. In order for your lawyer to resolve your case, he or she will need a large number of documents that only you can get. Your lawyer will also need to know what witnesses you intend to call if this matter were to go to trial.

Chances are, this entire process is going to be very demanding. Don't put it off. The sooner you start, the sooner it will be over. The sooner it is over, the cheaper your case may be. You have to treat this like a job and you have to start now. If you tend to procrastinate, you need to break that habit immediately.

25. What is Your Realistic Budget?

When it comes to war, you need ammo and in this case, your ammo is money. How much do you really want to throw at this case? Where will the money come from? In big divorce wars, the person with the most money usually comes out on top. If you don't have a lot of money to throw at the case, you have to tailor your strategy accordingly. Instead of rushing into court with a motion, you'll have to compromise and work with the other side on smaller issues. This way, your money is saved for the more important issues.

Keep in mind that your lawyer may not be able to tell you how much your divorce can cost. However, you need to understand how much you can spend.

VI. MEDIATION AND OTHER ADR AVAILABLE (ADR: ALTERNATIVE DISPUTE RESOLUTION)

26. Find Out What is Available in Your Area

Every state is different and in some states, divorce practice varies from court to court. As a result, some ADR options may be unique to certain areas. You need to understand what is available and whether any of those options are a good fit to win your case. You will also need to know when these options are available, how to prepare for them and how each will be handled. ADR options include mediation, arbitration and negotiation.

27. Mediation as an Alternative

Mediation as a complete alternative to divorce litigation is rarely a good idea in New Jersey but that doesn't mean it isn't the best option in other states. In New Jersey, divorce mediation is marketed as not just an alternative to a traditional divorce case but it is also marketed as an alternative to hiring a lawyer. That is a huge problem for me and not because I have some agenda to get lawyers more cases. Trust me, if a lawyer is good, he or she is already quite busy as it is. Furthermore, I have a mediation practice in addition to my divorce practice.

Instead, I hate to see people spend a lot of money to fix avoidable mistakes. Too many people take the cheap way out and hire a mediator only to have the entire situation blow up in their face at some point. The mediator cannot give you legal advice and thus, you should never settle your case without a lawyer helping you throughout the entire process. In addition, the process is usually done backwards whereby you mediate the divorce case and then file for divorce only after it is settled. That can lead to big problems.

This marketing of mediation also implies that the alternative is a nasty, expensive divorce where the lawyers will take all of your money. That is not even close to being true. More importantly, they don't tell you that there are numerous mediation options available, some of which are even forced upon you during a typical divorce case.

If you are going to choose mediation as an alternative to a traditional divorce, you should at least have a lawyer either with you during the mediation or to review the settlement agreement afterward. You should also make sure that there is some benefit to this or at least understand the risks involved. For some people, this is the right decision and my mediation clients enjoy the speed and cost effectiveness of the process.

28. Mediation as Part of the Divorce Case

As I indicated in #27, there are mediation options as part of a divorce case including some which you must attend. In some counties in New Jersey, there are at least three court mandated mediation sessions in a divorce case. The best part is, two of them are free and the other one is partially free. Thus, why pay a mediator when you can get one for free?

Even if your court doesn't have that or if you have to wait too long to get there, you can still hire a mediator to work through the issues in your case. Don't assume it's a sign of weakness because it's not. Divorce trials are a sign that the process has failed. The smartest business people working for Fortune 500 copies routinely negotiate, mediate and settle various disputes. While you need a lawyer that is ready to go to trial (i.e. war) you should try to avoid getting there.

29. Arbitration

Arbitration is a great alternative to trial. With arbitration, a neutral party such as an experienced lawyer or retired judge takes testimony from both sides in an informal setting such as a conference room. The arbitrator then issues a decision which is binding on both parties. Rules can be relaxed and the time period can be greatly sped up. This is because trials are formal and very lengthy. Most judges do not have the time to give you numerous trial days. For example, you could pay your lawyer to sit in court for seven hours just to get one hour of trial time in. So, 40 hours of trial could cost you 200 hours of time both in the court room and then outside the court room preparing for trial.

While you don't have to pay your judge, you have to pay the arbitrator and he or she can be expensive; probably more expensive than your lawyer. This cost can be split with your spouse is most circumstances. However, the informal nature and the speed of the process will help you lessen your legal fees. Again, you have to weigh the pros and cons of this option along with the costs compared to trial. Only your lawyer can tell you if arbitration is right for you and your case but you should at least discuss this issue to rule it in or out.

30. Negotiation

No matter what you do and no matter where your divorce is going to take place, negotiation in one or more forms will play a huge role in your divorce case. 9 out of 10 divorce cases are settled using negotiation. For some this may be obvious but it seems to me that a lot of people don't understand this concept. I often hear questions about the judge. What will the judge do? What will the judge think? Does the judge hate men or women? Truth is, the judge may have very little to do with your case unless you file a motion or go to trial.

Even if your case does go to trial, you will probably have settled at least some of your issues. Therefore, no matter how you look at it, you are going to have to negotiate and that means you will not get everything you want. However, if you defined winning properly, this will not be a problem for you.

Entire books have been written on negotiation so I won't go into detail here but I'll discuss numerous issues in the next chapter. As I have previously emphasized, you need to have realistic goals and a plan. What will you give up first, what will you trade for, and what is your walk away position? If you haven't discussed these issues with your lawyer, you are going into the entire process blind.

VII. NEGOTIATION STRATEGY

31. Timing is Everything

Negotiation is an art. You want to settle your case but you don't want to seem desperate. Thus, when you negotiate is just as important as how you negotiate. With most things in divorce, there is no one way to negotiate. Instead, your timing should be built into the plan.

For example, if a client says to me, 'I don't want the house; ask my husband's lawyer if he just wants to sell it'. I may not advise the other side of my client's desire if I think it is in her best interest to wait on that issue. What if the husband is out of the house and paying all the bills? How is it to my client's benefit to move out of the house now? What if we get stuck on another issue later and to compromise, I'll get my client agree to list the house for sale? Had I acted when she asked me, we would have lost that bargaining chip.

Of course, the timing for the husband is the other way around. In the same situation, maybe my client wants to sell now because she intends to buy another house that will be on the market in a few months? If she waits too long, that house might be sold. As you can see, each case differs from the next but the timing of when and how you negotiate is a very important part of your strategy.

32. Negotiations With Your Spouse

Before you start trying to negotiate with your spouse, talk to your lawyer first. I had a huge case where my client was forced to sign an agreement by his wife. He then hired me and the other lawyer from a huge firm threatened me with this agreement over and over again. Not being scared of big firms, we fought back and worked out the case without having to worry about this prior agreement. However, it definitely impacted the negotiations and it caused me to prepare to defend against a motion to enforce the agreement. That easily added several thousand dollars to the client's retainer.

The other problem with negotiating with your spouse is that you are too emotionally wrapped up in the case (even if you are following my earlier advice) and you probably have no real experience negotiating. Thus, you may wind up telling your spouse what the important issues are which your spouse's lawyer can later use as leverage.

Of course, settling some issues with your spouse may be a great way to resolving the entire case. It can also help do an end-run around your spouse's lawyer who could be blocking a settlement. Like anything, you should discuss this issue with your lawyer and receive guidance as to if you should negotiate and then what you will say.

33. Get All the Facts Before Starting

One of the biggest problems with negotiating divorce cases is when the parties cannot agree on the facts. You say that your spouse ran up the credit card debt on frivolous items while your spouse says that it was all for marital purposes. If no one has gone through the actual credit card statements, how can this issue ever be solved?

Of course, it's not always easy to know what issues you are going to get hung up on but there are ways to either avoid it or deal with it.

First, you should attempt to have all of the facts before you negotiate. This will obviously cut down on the number of factual disputes. Second, if a factual dispute occurs, don't get into a shouting match with your spouse. Instead, isolate exactly what is causing the dispute and what document or other piece of evidence will help resolve that dispute. Third, agree as to who will gather that evidence and when. Fourth, either move past that issue and resolve other issues or stop the negotiation.

34. Using Negotiation Statements

A negotiation statement is a document that your lawyer will use to lay out all of the disputed issues in the case, your position, the law on that topic and all the facts that support your assertions. At least, that's the correct way to do it. Too many lawyers are lazy and if they have to go to mediation or arbitration, they will just write up the issues. I write it up my statements to narrow down if not eliminate the factual and legal disputes that may arise.

For example, if I think that my client should get X, I have the case law and/or statute indicating why my client should get that just as if I am in front of the judge making my closing argument. If the dispute is over the purchase date of the house, there is a copy of the deed attached as an exhibit. I do this with all issues so that as soon as a dispute is raised, I point everyone to the appropriate exhibit and ask how I could be wrong. If there is a dispute as to the law, I point out what my research shows and I ask for the case law that is contrary to that position. That really boxes my adversary into a corner and as a result, their position is seriously weakened to the point where they may lack credibility.

If you are using a third person such as a mediator or an arbitrator, the negotiation statement will be given to that person. If you are just negotiating with the other side, your lawyer may not show it to them.

However, it is still just as useful because your lawyer cannot possibly remember every case or fact that supports your position. Portions of the statement or exhibits to it may be shared with the other side to resolve a dispute.

Without a negotiation statement, your lawyer is winging it and that is certainly no plan.

VIII. SETTLEMENT STRATEGY

35. Facts vs. Emotion

In my experience, most disputes during settlement are due to emotion and not facts. If you took my earlier advice, this shouldn't be a problem for you. If you didn't, you'll be more concerned with her keeping the expensive car that you really wanted instead of just looking at all of the assets as items to be valued and distributed. Who cares that he gets to keep all the furniture as long as you got something that is just as valuable? It's all just stuff. Don't worry about it and don't try to settle the case when you are emotional.

36. Fighting Solves Nothing

In your daily life, you don't see two grown adults screaming at each other over nonsense as if they are children. However, this happens quite often in divorce cases and I hate it when my clients do it. It tells me that my client is not listening to me and as a result, our entire plan may be in jeopardy.

You don't have to get the last word in and you don't have to fight fire with fire. Think about it this way, any idiot can get into a street fight but it's the wise person that knows it is better to walk away. Another way to look at is what is this fighting going to solve? Is it going to help you win your case? While I can't say much with absolute certainty, I can tell you that fighting will not help you settle your case. In fact, it will probably make things more difficult because both sides will dig in as they are now defending their pride in addition to defending their position.

If your spouse starts yelling at you during any settlement discussions, your best bet is to just walk away. If you remove yourself from the situation, who is left to fight?

37. Does Your Lawyer Tell You No?

Your lawyer should not be a yes man/woman. You should hear the word no and probably here it quite often. I tell my clients the truth whether they want to hear it or not. Some don't want to hear it. Luckily, I screen my prospective clients and as a result, when some people hear no, they don't hire me. I am far too busy to tell someone what they want to hear. I'll let someone else rip them off cause I'm not about to do it.

Of course, you are still the boss so your lawyer should still fight for you and go in that direction even if the lawyer doesn't think it's the best idea. Don't expect your lawyer to break any laws or rules though. That's where it stops. Also, your lawyer may put in writing that you have been advised that you are going in the wrong direction. Your lawyer needs to be covered if this move blows up in your face.

38. Move Around Logjams

It's not uncommon in settlement discussions to get stuck on an issue. I refer to these issues as a logjam because it can grind everything to a halt even if the other issues have nothing to do with it. If you really get stuck, the best way to move forward is to just work around the logjam. Table it for another day and try to resolve the other issues in the case. You'd be amazed how often resolving these unrelated issues helps to break the logjam. While a psychologist can probably explain the reasoning better than I can, it seems that there is a lot to be said for momentum. If you are making good progress and you have gotten used to the idea of compromising with your spouse, the attachment you had to that logjam issue lessens, and you are more likely to compromise on that issue.

Even if that issue remains, it's not really a logjam anymore as you've moved past it and settled all of your other issues. If you do have to go to trial, it will be much easier dealing with just that issue then the entire case.

IX. ALIMONY ISSUES

39. Money is Money

The dreaded A word. It's the worst thing about representing the higher income earner. No one wants to even hear about alimony, let alone pay it. This has to be the most emotionally charged issue in the case. You mean I have to pay her (or him in some cases) how much and for how long!!!!????? It can really make a case difficult to handle.

Sticking with the big theme in this book, you have to just look at alimony as money. It doesn't matter what you pay or to whom or why. It's just money. Who cares that she (or he) may get alimony? What can you really do about it except apply the law to the facts to keep your total payout in the divorce case as low as possible. Remember to treat this like a business transaction.

40. Understand Tax Implications

This issue gets lost on many clients and some lawyers. Alimony is tax-deductible to the paying spouse and taxable to the spouse that is receiving it. Depending on your tax bracket, that $20,000 in alimony will result in a deduction that means it will only be 17,500 after taxes since you are saving $2,500 on taxes you would have otherwise paid. If you take the emotion out of this issue, it becomes pretty easy to understand. If you are fixated on giving your spouse $20,000, it may be impossible to understand.

Likewise, if you are the spouse receiving alimony, you have to run all the numbers so that you understand that if you are getting $20,000 in alimony, you may net much less. Will that be enough to meet your needs?

41. Discuss all What If Scenarios

-What if you lose your job next year or get hurt?

-What if your spouse gets a good job?

-What if your spouse remarries?

-What if your spouse lives with someone but doesn't get married?

Failure to discuss every 'what if' scenario can put either side in a tough position down the road. If you don't understand these scenarios, you can shoot yourself in the foot. Also, your settlement agreement may leave you without the necessary protection.

Understanding your agreement is not simply knowing what you are getting, but it's also understanding how future events can impact the terms of the settlement.

42. Lump Sum vs. Period Payments

Now that you understand all of the different scenarios, you may want to discuss a lump sum buyout. What if you are dating someone and that person insists on getting married? If you are receiving alimony, that could be a big problem. What if your spouse gets sick and can't work? What if you want to retire early and not have to worry about monthly alimony payments? There are a number of reasons why a lump sum buyout may make sense.

Unfortunately for some, this isn't even an option but if it is, it should be explored. I have been able to get clients out of permanent alimony in exchange for a lump sum buyout which was the equivalent of just five years of alimony. That's a pretty nice deal, don't you think?

While it's not right for everyone, it's a conversation worth having. One important thing to consider is that alimony buyouts ensure that you don't have to worry about the other side filing a motion to increase, decrease or terminate the alimony payments.   Not having to worry about future legal bills is certainly a good thing.

43. Imputation of Income

You can't just work less (or not at all) and claim that you can't pay alimony or that you should get more alimony. If you are unemployed or not fully employed, your income will be imputed. That is, for purposes of calculating an alimony obligation, the court will pretend that you make a certain amount.

There are a number of ways to impute income from labor statistics to employment experts. If you are unemployed or underemployed, you will have to address this with your lawyer early on as it may take quite some time to put together your best argument.

X. CHILD SUPPORT

44. Know the Rules

When it comes time to calculate child support, you need to know the basics.

-How is it calculated?

-How is it paid?

-Will it increase or decrease over time?

-What if the other side doesn't pay?

-What should you look out for?

-When does it end?

Have these conversations with your lawyer now and you'll be more prepared for the future. Also, you need to plan for college. What are the laws in your state on this issue? How much will be enough in 5, 10, or 15 years? Besides speaking with your lawyer, a conversation with a financial adviser might be in order as well.

45. Have the Numbers

You need all of the numbers. If you don't have them, you'll be in the dark as to why you are paying that amount. You need to know how much you make and how much the other side makes. You also need to know how the child support figure was calculated. This way, if you ever have to see a lawyer about this issue in the future, you can show him or her exactly how the child support figure was determined.

46. When Will This Change?

That child support award will likely change but when? How? Is it automatic or do you have to do something? What if it does change? What can you do about it at that point? You need to have the answers to all of these questions.

47. What Does it Cover?

Child support doesn't cover everything so you need to understand when you should ask your ex-spouse for more money or what to do if your ex-spouse asks you for more money. If you don't understand what it covers or doesn't cover, you could be paying too much to your ex-spouse or not seeking contribution for an expense not covered by child support. If some of these expenses are predictable, you should spell them out in the settlement agreement to avoid any dispute in the future.

48. Child Support May be Used as Alimony

This drives a lot of people nuts. Child support is supposed to be for the child. However, it can be used to support the other parent one way or another. In most cases, the parent receiving child support doesn't have to spend it on certain items. Thus, a portion of your child support could be used on your spouse to get her hair done or to fix his motorcycle. There's not too much you can do about it in most cases.

Obviously if the other parent is not buying the child clothes because all of the child support is being spent on themselves, then that is a big problem. Discuss those issues with your lawyer.

49. When Does It End?

The answer to this question is different in every state. In some states, child support terminates automatically at a certain age. In New Jersey, only a judge can terminate child support which is called emancipation. New Jersey is one of the toughest states, and parents spend thousands litigating this issue. Regardless of what your state does, you need to know when it will end and if you need to do anything to make it end.

50. What About College?

In some states, a parent does not have to contribute to a child college. In New Jersey, both parents have to contribute to a child's college even if both parents object! In other words, New Jersey guarantees that your parents will have to send you to college if they are financially able to do so. On top of college expenses, child support will continue. Imagine having to pay alimony, college expenses and child support all at the same time? That's not a fun conversation to have with your client, trust me.

If you live in a state where this is not an issue, you may still want to discuss this issue and possibly make it part of your settlement. Surely you want the best for your child. Is it possible to take some assets and put them in an account to fund your child's education even if the court won't force you to do so?

XI. THE MARITAL RESIDENCE

51. Don't Get Attached to It

The house is an asset like any other. However, it probably has a ton of emotional attachment. You cannot get hung up on the house from an emotional level. Look at the facts. There are two issues that you have to consider. First, should the house be sold or kept by one party? Second, if the house is sold, where will you go, especially if you have children?

If the house is kept by one party, you may be forced to refinance if the mortgage is in both of your names. That can be difficult depending on how much the house is worth and how much you make. If there is a lot of equity, the other side needs to get their fair share one way or another. How is that going to happen? If the house is underwater, do you do a short sale or do you live rent free for a few years while you wait for a foreclosure?

If you are thinking about moving, you need to figure out where you are going to go. Will you rent or own? Even if the house is underwater, is the mortgage cheaper than renting? What if you have 4 giant dogs; what landlord is going to accept that? Can you keep the children in the same school system? Do you have to because they have special needs or talents?

Instead of saying you want the house just because you are attached, analyze the issue by considering the points asked above in addition to others that may be relevant to your situation.

52. Use a Good Real Estate Agent

There's nothing I hate more than a bad real estate agent. Too many of them take the approach that if they sign up enough listings, some will sell and they will make money. However, they are not really doing anything for you. There is no real plan. Instead, they are just hoping that someone comes along and buys your house at some point.

Real estate agents are in a tough spot. They are a dime a dozen and if they try to talk sense into a client, the client may walk and hire someone else thus losing out on a sale. As a result, I find real estate agents to be bigger yes men/women than any other profession.

You need a real estate agent that will give it to you straight. They will tell you how much your house is worth and what it should be listed for, when and how it will be shown, and when prices should be dropped. I don't care how bad the real estate market is, houses do sell. You just need a plan.

If you have an open house that is well attended and you don't have any offers, there is a problem and you need to find out what it is. Now it could be that the people looking at your home were suspects and not prospects. That's the fault of their real estate agent, not you. However, if these people were prospects and they didn't make an offer, your agent should be getting some feedback. Is there something they don't like about your house? Is there too much competition? Are you priced too high? The problem needs to be identified and corrected.

With many people using the Internet to find houses, the right price is important. $600,000 vs. $599,999 might not seem like a big deal but if someone is searching for houses under $600,000 that could keep you out of the search results. You don't want to chase the market either. Have a plan as to when to reduce the listing price, why and by how much. Sitting at the same listing price for months on end is hardly a strategy unless you have a very unique house where it's hard to find the right buyer. For 99% of people selling a house, this is not a problem.

I am telling you all of this not to give you real estate advice but to give you an idea as to what a good real estate agent may tell you. Just like your divorce case, you need a plan and your agent is the expert that should give it to you. Putting a sign in front of the house and having a few open houses is not a plan. Neither is blaming the market. I know some real estate agents that are constantly selling houses regardless of the market.

53. Scrutinize the Appraisal

When the house is not going to be sold, it needs to be valued. While you can get a real estate agent to do a comparative market analysis, the best evidence as to the home's value is an appraisal. There are companies that specialize in appraisals and they will look at your home along with other similar homes in the area that have sold called *comps* in order to arrive at a value.

Some appraisals are good in that they find good comps, they scrutinize the house and they provide analysis. Other appraisals are not so good. Sometimes they don't bother to go into the house and without doing that, they could miss important upgrades. Others may use listings as comps which are not helpful since anyone can list a house at any price they want. It doesn't mean those houses are actually worth that price. If the analysis is faulting or even lacking, the whole appraisal may be subject to scrutiny by either side.

If you are going to get your own appraisal to counter one that you don't agree with, that appraisal must attack the first one and point out exactly what was wrong. Without that, it's just two people with different opinions. How could a judge possibly figure out which one is better on their own?

XII. PERSONAL PROPERTY

54. Don't Get Your Lawyer Involved

There is no way your personal belongings and average household goods are worth that much that you should get your lawyer involved. At trial, these items will be valued at pennies on the dollar. So that furniture set that cost you $5,000? The court may value it at $500. I tell my clients to just work with their spouse to divide everything evenly but don't get hung up on making sure that you get one fork for every spoon that your spouse is getting.

Focus on what's important and don't worry about the rest of that stuff. If neither of you want it, have a garage sale and then use the money to pay off a joint credit card or split the money. In the end, the most common way to resolve disputes about personal belongings with little value is to just flip for it. It sounds crazy but what sounds even crazier is spending $5,000 over something worth $500.

55. Deal With this Before Divorce is Over

While this doesn't need to be put in your settlement agreement (although it could be), you don't want any issues hanging out there after the divorce is over. The divorce should end all issues between the two of you. Thus, don't assume that you will get divorced and then figure this out. That's how trouble starts and you want to avoid as much trouble as you can. A simple letter between the two lawyers can confirm that all personal items have been distributed.

XIII. CHILD CUSTODY

56. Know the Law

Are you noticing a pattern here yet? You must understand what child custody means in your state.

-What does it mean to be the primary custodian also known as the custodial parent?

-What does it mean to be the parent of alternate residence?

-What does joint legal custody entail in your state?

-Who has to do what?

Not only must you understand these concepts but you must insist that your property settlement agreement be specific so that there is no confusion as to the rights and responsibilities of each parent.

57. Consider Practical Reality

The children are not pawns in your war against your spouse so don't treat them as such. They are not items to be divided and you don't need to count up each minute to see who has what time. How much time can you actually spend with them given your work schedule? Like many things in this book, I know this may sound like common sense but you'd be amazed at how many people are fighting to get more time with the kids when they really don't have the time to spend with them!

You also have to consider the practical reality of the law which some people don't want to hear. Most states will ensure that both parents share some time with the children no matter how bad of a parent they may be. As one judge put it, children are not entitled to A+ parents under the law; the law only ensures that they have D- parents. So, unless you demonstrate a danger to the children, you have to accept that the court will give the other parent some parenting time. Thus, fighting for no parenting time might be a waste of time and money.

58. Put Everything in Writing

This is where so many people fail. Everything must be spelled out in your divorce settlement and if your lawyer doesn't insist on it, you must. Now keep in mind, if you swap a day here and there with your spouse, you don't have to run to court every time to amend your settlement. However, if there is going to be some type of big fundamental change, it must be in writing. You have to think about the worst case scenario. The purpose of having court orders is to be able to understand and enforce your rights. If you don't have it in writing, it will be difficult to enforce. And when I say put it in writing, I am almost always talking about a court order in one form or another.

People often ask me, 'what are my rights'. My reply is that without a court order, you don't have many. Thus, get it in righting and have the court sign it.

59. Using Parenting Coordinators

For those hotly contested cases, you may want to consider using a parenting coordinator. They may have different names in other states but the concept is the same: a neutral person whom will work with the two of you on an as needed basis to resolve parenting time disputes. While this person does not work for free, whatever their cost is will be much cheaper than hiring an attorney to go to court to resolve the case.

60. Change in Circumstances

Courts do not want you to keep coming back every few days to try to change your custody/parenting time order. As a result, one basic concept perhaps across every state is *change of circumstances*. That is, if you want to change the custody or parenting time provisions of a court order, you have to show that something has changed. This prevents a litigant from complaining about buyer's remorse or from filing a motion just because they feel like it.

This is another concept that should be discussed with your lawyer.

-What will you need to show if you want to change the court order?

-What will the other side need to show?

-How could you strengthen a possible motion between now and then?

-How could you defeat a possible motion filed by your spouse in the future?

61. When Can Children Make Their Own Decision?

There is no universal age where children can make their own decisions as to where they want to live. Some states may have a set age, while others don't. It's possible that a 15 year old could be more mature than a 16 year old, and thus, the 15 year old will have more control than that 16 year old. One concept is clear though, the older the child is, the more weight the judge gives to their preference. Unless there are some unique circumstances, most judges do not want to tell a 17 year old who to live with.

Be sure to factor that in when fighting for custody. I've seen people file motions to get custody of a 17 year old and this has always been a waste of time; at least in my experience.

62. Dealing with Parental Alienation

Parental alienation is a widespread epidemic that is largely not discussed in society. Every single week I get not one but several calls from a parent who complains that they have no relationship with their children. As a result, they are seeking to end child support because they don't want to pay for a child that doesn't speak with them. Not enough people call a lawyer to get back into their children's lives at the first sign of trouble.

A spouse hell bent on parental alienation is a very difficult foe and the case will not be easy. The best way to prevent alienation is to fight it. Set the tone in the divorce case itself. Assert yourself, no matter if you are the father or the mother as the parent you want to be, which I would assume would be a very involved parent. You have to make sure that you are involved in every aspect of this child's life and that you have a rock solid court order in place to enforce your rights.

As I previously indicated, you have to know what to do in the event that you need to enforce your rights. After the divorce, your ex-spouse may test you. You have to fight back hard and fast. If you don't, you are teaching the other parent that you are a pushover and they will continue to test you more and more. As time goes on, your relationship with your child will lessen eventually leading to resentment. At the first sign of danger you must take action.

Besides taking action, you can't give up. No matter how bad it looks and no matter how long it takes, you have to keep fighting. Too many people wait until alienation already sets in and the fight to get back into the child's life is a long one but it can be won.

XIV. LITIGATING FINANCIAL ISSUES

63. Closely Held Business

These cases can be a real nightmare. However, you can make this nightmare a little easier by recognizing that this is going to be an issue from the start and then have your attorney work on it ASAP. It's rare for a small, closely held business to accurately report income. You'll often see six figure gross incomes with only $20,000 reported as profit. Keep in mind that this may be perfectly legal but you cannot allow your spouse to claim that they make only $20,000 per year. There are many tax write offs that should be added back into that spouse's income to figure out how much they really make.

There may also be a lot of cash payments that go unreported. If this matter is presented to a judge, the judge may be forced to report you both to the IRS. That is really going to compound your problems. First, you have to uncover all of these cash payments to figure out how much the business is worth. This is often done with a forensic accountant. Second, if there are potential IRS issues, you may want to consider hiring an arbitrator to decide your case to avoid being reported to the IRS. They may not be bound by the same laws that the judges are.

Regardless of the tactic you take, having a lawyer that starts to work on this complicated issue sooner rather than later can go a long way to resolving this issue in your favor.

64. Dealing with Under the Table Income

A spouse that gets paid under the table is even trickier than dealing with a closely held business sometimes; especially if they are paid in cash. Your lawyer could subpoena your spouse's employer to testify at a deposition but the employer may invoke his/her right to remain silent. Your spouse may even get fired at that point which could then backfire on you.

Of course, if you take this aspect of the case to trial, the court may report you to the IRS as I mentioned previously. Thus, you are in a real catch-22 here. There are a number of ways to deal with this and you should discuss them with your lawyer. While the cash payments may be tough to prove if they are not deposited in the bank, the martial lifestyle should be fairly easy to prove. The bills are paid, the house is maintained and as a family, you live a decent lifestyle. You haven't racked up a ton of credit card debt either so the money had to come from somewhere. Figuring out your average monthly budget subtracted by your income should show a pretty accurate picture of how much your spouse makes.

65. Using Forensic Accountants

As I have previously mentioned, forensic accountants may be necessary in your case. Depending upon the complexity of the financial issues, this expert could cost $3000, $15,000 or even more. While you want to have all of the facts before you even attempt to settle your case, you don't want to jump at the idea of hiring a forensic accountant because of the cost involved. Make this decision carefully.

If you are not satisfied with the forensic accountant's report, you need to meet with your lawyer to come up with a plan to deal with it. You may have to hire your own expert which could cost even more money. Regardless of your thoughts on the report, you should review it carefully with your lawyer. Just because they are experts does not mean they don't make mistakes. I've dealt with many experts that did not write their report correctly. One even admitted under questioning that their testimony should not be considered by the court!

66. Discovery Tools

One of the most common questions I get is how my client is going to get access to various bills, accounts, payments, etc. For the most part, the answer is pretty simple: discovery. Discovery requires that all parties put all of their cards on the table. There are no Perry Mason moments where a mysterious witness comes into the court room to surprise everyone. Discovery allows almost the entire trial to be scripted which prevents most trials from occurring in the first place. You need to make sure that your lawyer is using as many discovery tools as possible.

The average discovery tools are interrogatories, notice to produce, requests for admissions, subpoenas and depositions. Interrogatories are a set of questions, sometimes hundreds, which ask about numerous issues, some of which do not even apply to your case. Your spouse will have to answer these questions and then swear that the answers are true. The answers may be open-ended or yes or no with a follow up explanation requested. A request for admission is a list of statements asking that the party admit or deny each statement. A notice to produce is a request to produce a document although some document requests can be made in interrogatories as well. Subpoenas are a legal request for a specific document, often to a third party such as a bank.

Once your lawyer digests all of that information, he or she may decide to depose your spouse. This is rare in most divorce cases as it is largely unnecessary unless the case appears headed for trial. You've probably seen a deposition on TV or in a movie. Both lawyers and both parties are in a conference room with a court reporter. The parties and other witnesses can be questioned and everything they say is sworn testimony just as if it was taken in a court room. However, there is no judge or jury present so the lawyer is free to ask more open-ended questions to get information. At an eventual trial, these questions will be streamlined to get to the point.

Not all of these discovery tools will be needed for your case but it is important to understand what tools are out there and why some are being used in your case, while others are not.

67. Look at Your Post-Divorce Life

Although this is #67, it ties in with number 1. Not only do you need to unravel the financial issues between you and your spouse, but you need to think about the financial issues that you will encounter post-divorce.

-Where will you live?

-What will your housing expenses be?

-What financial habits will you change?

- How will you invest your money?

-Is bankruptcy an option? Will you have enough to survive?

-How will you pay off your lawyer (very important!)?

Chances are your divorce will have a dramatic impact on your finances, at least for a period of time. No matter how easy your case is, it's cheaper for two people to live together than apart 90% or more of the time. If you don't plan, you may win your case but you will still lose out in the end because you will be caught off guard when reality hits you.

XV. LITIGATING CHILD CUSTODY ISSUES

68. Mentally Prepare for War

You tried to settle your custody issues but it's come down to an all-out war. You have to get yourself prepared mentally because it's going to get ugly. If the other side has a decent lawyer, they are going to stop at nothing to run you over. You cannot let every little thing upset you. It amazes me how a simple letter filled with nonsense from the other lawyer only addressed to me can send even the most rational client into a frenzy. I often want to ask, 'so you teach your child sticks and stones . . . , but that doesn't apply to you?'. No matter who says what to whom, you can't get upset. If the other side is saying bad things about you in a letter sent just to your lawyer, treat that as a blessing. The moron is tipping their hand and instead of getting upset, you have to focus on deflecting the mud! (See #76).

If you can get yourself mentally prepared for all of the nonsense that will come your way, you will really be ahead of the game and it will be easier for your lawyer to win your case.

69. Consider Post-Divorce Life

No matter what happens with the custody issues in your case, the two of you will still be the parents of these children. Thus, whether your case ultimately goes to trial or is settled, you have to think about the long term. Discuss this issue with your lawyer. While the court cannot issue advisory opinions, you have to at least voice your concerns to your lawyer who may in turn voice them to the court. You don't want to go through a whole trial just to be back in court a few months later to deal with issues you should have raised earlier.

There is no limit to the questions you may want answers to, but they can start with "how will we...", "what if _____ happens", "when is it time to _____". A few examples include: "what if the children are sick, do I have to give them to the other side?"; "what if I want to move"; "what if my spouse has a boyfriend/girlfriend sleep over", "what do I have to tell the other parent?"; "how will we communicate?".

70. Keep a Journal

Divorce and custody wars can drag on. You don't want to be in a position of testifying about something that happened at the start of the divorce case two years ago. With all that has gone on, you won't have the best recollection. I tell all my clients to keep a journal. There is no magic to it, it's whatever you want it to be. When something happens, write it down with as much info as possible. You can then come into court and testify with great accuracy. As a result, you'll have greater credibility and in the end, that's what this case will likely come down to. As always, discuss this issue with your lawyer.

71. Line up Your Witnesses

A judge's worst nightmare is a he-said, she-said trial. Despite taking an oath to tell the truth, most witness shade the truth if not all out lie, and everyone knows it. Thus, it's hard for a judge to figure out who is telling the truth and who isn't. That's why every important fact needs to be supported several different ways. I always go for overkill. If the issue is the color of the car, I'm going to have my client testify, bring in a picture of the car and three different witnesses that can testify that the car is the color my client says it is.

You don't want to wait until it's too late to find your witnesses, see if they remember and then ask them to pick a side. Nail them down right away and take statements from them. You'll quickly find out who is on your side and who is against you. Your lawyer will guide you through this process.

72. What's on the Internet?

The fact that I have to even mention this point demonstrates that fog of war that occurs during divorce or custody litigation. If you are even thinking about divorce, you need to sanitize the Internet as much as possible. I realize everyone hates to do this, but I would pretty much delete your Facebook account all together and Google yourself to death. Any post or picture can be taken out of context. That picture of you pretending to chug a beer was funny at the time but it can be used now to claim that you are an alcoholic.

Also, you need to stay off the Internet. It amazes me how naive some people are but you have to assume that if you post anything on the Internet no matter where it is or how locked down you think you have your profile, someone will find it. Once the divorce is over, it's not my problem, but don't create problems for yourself. It's not important.

73. Gathering Additional Evidence?

Some clients want to be overly helpful. As a result, they will break into cars, filing cabinets, plant hidden recording devices, etc. You hired a lawyer for a reason, remember? Follow his or her advice. Don't play lawyer, and whatever you do, don't play lawyer and investigator at the same time! Whether it's recording your spouse, breaking into something, or even asking someone else if they will testify for you, don't do anything until your lawyer tells you to. If you gather evidence on your own, it could cause a world of problems for you. Remember that you have no idea what you are doing or what is important.

74. Using Experts

Experts are very helpful in a variety of situations. However, they are usually fairly expensive. Luckily, most divorce cases will not need expensive experts. Don't confuse a service with an expert. For example, most divorce cases will use some sort of appraisal to determine the value of the house (unless it's going to be sold). That's not really an expert in the traditional sense (although there are certain complex real estate issues calling for one).

Instead, experts in a divorce case typically are called in to analyzable issues such as mental health, substance abuse, custody, tracing hidden money, valuing a closely held business, or determining a spouse's potential income. Of course, there are others.

If you think an expert is needed in your case, discuss this with your lawyer. Topics for discussion should be whether or not to hire one, which one to hire, when, how much, who will pay for it, and what is the goal?

75. Throwing Mud

Unfortunately, mud has to be thrown sometimes if you want to win. If you present a case where both parents are fit, there are no complaints, and both have been actively involved in raising the children, you are going to have a tough time convincing the judge that you should get the children over your spouse. Now if you add in all the *mud* that you can throw, such as arrests, domestic violence, alcohol use, drug use, and work place issues, then you have a much better chance.

Of course what is mud and what is garbage can only be determined by your lawyer. It's your job to present everything to your lawyer and let him or her decide. If you take your emotions out of it, this should be easy. If you don't, you will get hung up on issues that may be irrelevant such as adultery. Some clients just can't wrap their head around the fact that in New Jersey, adultery is almost always 100% irrelevant.

When to throw mud is also important. I get cases sometimes where the adversary sets forth their whole case in the divorce complaint when it is 100% irrelevant. It doesn't need to be there. The only thing that lawyer is doing is charging his or her client more money for drafting the complaint and then giving the other side an idea as to what they need to defend against.

That happened in one case I had around the time I was writing this book. The other side called my client an alcoholic and claimed she had mental health issues. So what did I do about it? Keep reading.

76. Deflecting Mud Thrown at You (Deal with it Early)

This is one of the most important aspects of divorce litigation and this is where most lawyers fail their clients. When mud is thrown at your client, a lawyer needs to deflect it right away. Of course, this is hard to do when it is a total surprise. Fortunately, most lawyers are not that smart as I previously indicated.

Going back to my example in #75, the other lawyer pretty much gave me his playbook. From day one, I set my client up with several evaluations and I told her to get a metric ton of character letters. By the time this issue reached court about a month later, we were fully prepared. We won the emergency motion that the other side filed and the other lawyer pretty much ceded custody to my client. So much for a long, drawn out custody battle. Had I not been tipped off as to their strategy, we would not have been prepared. My client could have temporarily lost custody and it would have been very tough (and expensive) to get the children back. This is very similar to the issue I discussed at the beginning of this book.

Thus, the key is to try and figure out if the other side will be throwing any mud and smoke them out as to what mud they will be throwing as early as possible. You then need to deflect it so that it does not become an issue in your case. A skilled lawyer should already have a battle plan drawn up for this.

XVI. TRIAL

77. Limit the Issues

Judges are people too. I think most people, including most lawyers, forget that sometimes. What is easier to handle, a case with three primary issues or a case with 20 issues? The answer is clear so why would you take a case to trial with 20 issues? How could you possibly be so far apart on all 20 issues? In my experience, most cases boil down to just a handful of issues and it is rarely more than three. Thus, even if you can't settle your entire case, settle as many issues as possible.

A three issue trial will be faster and cheaper. Your arguments on these big issues will receive more time and attention from both your lawyer and the judge. Focus, on all sides, will make for a much better presentation. At the very least, you're lawyer will make a record that will be much easier to follow in the event of an appeal.

78. Using Stipulations

A stipulation is an agreement that both parties agree on a certain fact. For example, if both parties agree that the husband made $100,000 in 2012, then the parties would stipulate as to that fact. There should be a ton of stipulations since again, your case should only boil down to a handful of issues and even with those issues, only some facts will be disputed.

Stipulations also make the judge and your lawyer more focused on the important issues. Again, it also makes for a clean record. More importantly, you may actually annoy the judge by having your lawyer go on for hours with testimony that is largely uncontested. I've actually seen this happen where the judge kept asking the lawyer on the other side why most of these facts were not stipulated to. Her answer was, 'I don't know'. While it may be totally unrelated, I did win the trial. However, I can't help but realize that I was more focused on the disputed issues while she felt the need to discuss everything.

Besides all of the above, stipulations will make the trial go much faster which means that you will save a ton of money! Thus, you should insist that your lawyer enter into as many stipulations as possible.

79. Do You Have a Strategy?

I realize this sounds crazy, but you would be amazed at how many lawyers go into trial with absolutely no strategy whatsoever. They are really just winging it. When I am in trial, everything I do has a purpose. If I scratch my eye, I do it for a reason! No really, I am that focused! Why isn't your lawyer that focused?

Since you don't want to wait until you get to court to find out that your lawyer doesn't have a strategy, discuss that well ahead of time. In fact, trial strategy should be discussed in general terms at the beginning of the case. Planning in advance for trial is one of the best ways to avoid trial. It's one of the reasons why we don't have to do a ton of them.

Since most of the trial will already be scripted through the discovery process, a very specific trial strategy should be discussed right before trial. Every lawyer has their own strategy so there is no right way to do this. However, topics to be covered may include what witnesses to call, what documents to present, what to say, how to say it, and how to respond to cross examination. A big part of this is taking all of the information gathered in discovery and whittling down to the important items and presenting it in an organized format. Speaking of which . . .

80. Is Your Lawyer Organized?

I swear I'm not making this stuff up. I have been in cases where one of the lawyers shows up to trial with a stack of papers wrapped together in a rubber band. There's no file, folders, tabs or anything else that would even somewhat resemble organization. You should see these people try to handle a trial. When they need a document, it takes them several minutes to shuffle through this giant mess of papers. I don't know how these judges keep a straight face. I wouldn't have my time wasted because they are unprepared but thankfully for them, I'm not a judge.

Your concern is more important than just having your time wasted. You want to win! If your lawyer is not organized, your chances of success will go way down. If your lawyer consistently shows up to the court appearances leading up to trial with a giant stack of papers, then there is a good chance that he or she is not organized. The better way to tell is to ask. Meet with your lawyer before trial and ask to be shown how he or she is organized.

The primary way to be organized for trial is to have a trial binder. The trial binder should have all of the evidence organized in some logical format such as by witness or by issue. Most questions should be written out. The opening statement should also be written out. A draft of a closing argument should be done as well. Some judges also want trial briefs which are memos that lay out the contested issues along with the facts and law that supports your position. Even if this isn't required, it should still be done so that you and your lawyer understand the facts and law that will be argued in your case.

81. Settlement Discussions During Trial

Don't be surprised if settlement discussions continue through trial. It's not a sign of weakness and you should always be open to settlement discussions. In fact, some cases settle after trial. Once both sides have seen how the case has gone, they may feel less strong about their respective positions. A good judge can telegraph to the lawyers that they should settle one issue or another because the court's decision might be bad for both of them.

Of course, you don't want to have your lawyer begging the other side to settle the case to avoid a trial. This will seem weak and lawyers can smell fear like sharks smell blood. Instead, the discussions should come naturally when the time is right, if at all. That's different in each case and it may never happen. The bottom line is that you should be open to the idea of settling your case even though you are in the middle of a trial.

82. Relax

Trial can really provoke some anxiety. For probably the first time in your life, you have to get on the witness stand and testify. Everyone is looking at you. Even worse, in a few minutes, this other lawyer that works for your spouse is going to do everything he or she can to chew you up, spit you out and make you look stupid in the process.

If you are not relaxed, you are going to bomb. You have to remain focused with your eye on the prize at all times. All of your fear has to leave you. Hopefully, your lawyer has prepared you to death and you will be ready for anything. But no matter how much your lawyer prepares you, he or she cannot make you relax. I've prepared clients till I was blue in the face only to ask them the question, 'so what color was the car' to which they responded 'Thursday'. Ugh. After they testify I ask them, what happened because just five minutes before that, they knew the answer to that question. It's always the same answer, stage fright.

Finally, I don't suggest using medication to relax. This opens you up to a world of problems, especially if your mental health is at issue. If you think you need to take something to calm you down, ask your lawyer first.

83. Time Frame and Cost of Trial

When you are thinking about trial and even when you are going through the trial itself, always factor in the time frame and the cost. Except for custody and parenting time issues, almost all other issues in the case have a monetary value even if they are not liquid. Your position should be able to be reduced to a total dollar figure and your spouse's position should have one too, even if you are the one that has to figure it out. The difference between the two is how far apart you are and in essence, that is the number you are fighting over. Let's call this the trial figure for now. For example, after totaling up your position on all of the financial issues such as the house, the cars, support issues, etc., your best case scenario is worth $350,000. The settlement offer proposed by your spouse totals $300,000. Therefore, you are essentially going to trial over this difference, which is $50,000.

Now, factor in how long the trial will take and as a result, how much it will cost. We will call this the cost figure. This figure should be much smaller than the trial figure. The closer your cost figure is to your trial figure, the more likely you are seriously doing something wrong. All of this should be pointed out by your lawyer. If not, he or she may be trying to rip you off. Using the example above, it will cost you $40,000 to fight over $50,000. Your best case scenario is now only worth $10,000. If the other side gets their best case scenario you will not only lose the difference of the $50,000 you were originally fighting over but you have now lost an additional $40,000 bringing your total loss to $90,000. Put another way, if you go to trial, your downside is far greater than your upside.

Of course, this assumes that you are not going to trial already over non-monetary issues such as custody or parenting time. Those figures cannot be ascribed a monetary figure and should not figure into this analysis. In order to properly determine how much trial will cost, you will need to back out the costs for trial over those other issues. For example, if the entire trial will cost $40,000 but only half of that time will be spent dealing with monetary issues, than the trial cost is only $20,000. Using the previous example, this changes your upside to $30,000 and decreases your downside to $70,000. Using this example, I would still encourage the client to settle the monetary issues so that the trial can solely focus on these other more important issues.

Once you perform this analysis, or better yet, once you insist that your lawyer perform same, you may realize that you are risking thousands of dollars to net almost nothing and potentially lose much more. Maybe you should give settlement another chance.

84. Appeal Process

If you lose any portion of the trial, you can then file an appeal. The appeal process is different in every state, but a few basics are universal. Everything said during the trial and everything admitted into evidence is *the record*. This is important to understand because an appeal is not a do-over. Instead, it is a review by a higher court. Once the record is provided to the appellate court, lawyers for both sides will submit legal briefs. A panel of judges, who you may never see in person, will review the record along with legal briefs from both sides. Oral argument may be requested or they may just do everything through the mail. The panel of judges will then issue a decision. If they affirm the trial court, you lose. If they reverse the trial court you may win outright or the case may be sent back to the trial court or a different trial court for further proceedings. Thus, after a trial and an appellate process, all you may win is an opportunity to do the trial all over again!

85. Standard of Review / Odds

When evaluating whether or not to file an appeal, you must understand the standard of review. Because family court cases are so complicated, most appellate courts give special deference to the trial courts hearing these cases. As a result, the appellate court will not second guess the trial judge. Instead, you may have to show that the court abused its discretion which is a tough standard to meet. Of course, there are different standards of review for different issues and each State has their own laws.

This standard of review will allow your lawyer to give you some idea as to your odds of winning. For example, in New Jersey, if someone wants to appeal a trial and the trial court based it's decision largely upon the credibility of a witness (or lack thereof) attacking such a ruling may be very difficult. On the other hand, if you are attacking a procedural issue, you may have much better luck.

Thus, before you rush off to file an appeal, consider your odds of success with an emphasis on the standard of review.

86. Time Frame and Cost of Appeal

As if the trial wasn't expensive enough, get ready to pay even more for an appeal. Between ordering the transcripts, all the copies that need to get made, postage and the filing fee, you are probably looking at several thousand dollars. Then your lawyer has to review the transcript again, write a brief, review the other side's brief, write a reply and possibly go to court for oral argument. This is a ton of work which means a ton of money. Be sure to get a good idea as to this cost from your lawyer.

Again, every jurisdiction is different but appeals take time. Discuss this issue with your lawyer and decide if the time frame makes an appeal pointless. Don't be shocked if your lawyer says that the appeal process could take one to two years (or even longer).

XVII. DRAFTING THE SETTLEMENT

87. Must be Comprehensive

Settlement agreements must be as comprehensive as possible. Nothing can be left out and details cannot be left to the imagination. Every tiny little detail must be spelled out. Why? See my example in #89 for a real horror story, but the bottom line is that if you don't spell everything out, it could blow up in your face and leave you unprotected.

88. Include the Why

Often left out of many agreements is the why. What if both lawyers in the case retire next year, move to an island in the Pacific and are completely off the grid. No one will be able to ask them why the settlement agreement was drafted the way it was. No one is going to take your word for it, especially since your ex-spouse will probably have a different take on what the agreement means. So, how do you expect a judge to know why you set things up like this?

Consider this example. The husband pays wife $90,000 and she waives her right to alimony, his pension, annuity, and stock account. The husband waives his right to his wife's retirement account and the parties split the house equally. Reading this all together, it may seem obvious that the $90,000 is a buyout for all of those other assets and in exchange for leaving the wife's retirement untouched. What if I told you that the parties were only married for a month? His wife wouldn't have much of an alimony claim then, huh? What if I told you that the husband's assets are all premarital? Why is he paying her $90,000 then? To make this even more complicated, those issues may be found on different pages amongst other issues in an agreement that could be 15, 25 or 40 pages!

Your lawyer should be connecting the dots and explain why everything is being done. The $90,000 is in exchange for the wife waiving her interest in the husband's assets. The waiver of alimony is a mutual waiver because of the length of marriage and the lack of disparity in the parties' income. Or the wife is waiving alimony because she is living with her boyfriend. Whatever it is, discuss how to explain to someone reviewing this case in the future as to why you are settling the case this way.

89. Examine all What If Scenarios

You need your settlement agreement to be iron clad. To achieve this, run through all the *what if* scenarios. Your spouse agrees to do something, but what if . . . ? Consider this horror story.

The parties agree to list their house for sale. The husband will pay for carrying costs of house. He does not have to pay alimony until the house is sold.

Let's run through the what if's here.

-What if the house is listed too high?

-When will the house be lowered in price?

-What is the time frame for selling this house?

-What if the listing agreement expires?

-What if the husband stops paying for the house?

That's exactly what happened here. The house was never lowered in price, the listing agreement expired without the house selling and the husband stopped paying the mortgage.

The husband is in a great position here. Although he is not paying the carrying costs, he technically doesn't have to pay alimony since the house hasn't sold. Now the wife is in a tough spot because without alimony, she doesn't have money for a lawyer to fight this case. She lets it slide for a while and now she is being foreclosed on. If she had a better agreement, they could have appointed a receiver who would have worked to make sure the house was sold on time thus avoiding all of these problems. Even if the husband refused to pay alimony, he would have at least started racking up arrears.

Don't be like the wife in this scenario. Consider all the what if scenarios.

90. Read it Carefully at Least 10 Times (Have Others Read It)

Another problem I see often is that litigants will go back to their agreement a few weeks after they are divorced only to realize that something was left out or that an issue is vague. You need to read this line by line at least 10 different times. Have other people read it to, but make sure those people are not emotionally involved in your case. You need to make sure you think of everything, have read everything and that you understand everything.

91. Ask Many Questions

In order to understand the agreement, you should ask a lot of questions. Take your copy and mark it up. Take notes. Write down questions. Go through it with your lawyer line by line. There is no such thing as a stupid question. Understand every little word. Why was something included? Why was something left out? Why was it worded this way? What happens if something goes wrong? What if I make a mistake? You should have a lot of questions for your lawyer.

92. Vacating a Settlement Agreement

So you settled your case but something happened and you want to blow it up and start over. If you already went to court and had the judge sign off on your divorce case, this could be very difficult to do. At your final divorce hearing, you may be asked a series of questions about your understanding of the settlement. These questions are designed to make it almost impossible for you to ever come back and vacate the settlement. This is why it so important to do it right the first time.

Of course, if you think you have valid grounds to vacate the agreement, don't hesitate to contact your lawyer to discuss that. If your lawyer says that there is nothing you can do, you may want to run this issue by another lawyer. Your divorce lawyer may have made a mistake and may not want to admit that. However, if this new lawyer says you can vacate the agreement, understand exactly why that is, what will happen in that event and how much it may cost to finish the case from there.

XVIII. POST DIVORCE MOTIONS

93. Modifying Support Obligations

One of the most common post-divorce motions is a motion to modify either child support or alimony. Although each jurisdiction is different, modifying alimony may be tough. If your spouse has been remarried or if they hit the lottery, it may be an easier motion. If you are just tired of paying alimony or your new paramour is tired of you sending a lot of your money to your ex each month, these are not good reasons. Your settlement agreement is the first place to look as to whether or not you can file a motion to modify your alimony obligation. If that is silent (meaning you didn't follow my earlier advice) you need to see what the law is in your state. Either way, discuss this issue with your lawyer.

Modifying child support is much easier. Whereas alimony is usually a product of contract, child support is a product of law. The universal standard of modifying child support is changed circumstances. In other words, at the time the child support was set (in this case, the end of the divorce case), the situation pertaining to you, your ex, or both of you was one thing and now that situation has changed. As a result, child support should be modified or terminated all together.

Some of these motions are easy while others are complex. Each state and each case is different. Your agreement may give you some guidance but it may not include everything. Regardless of whether you are paying child support or receiving it, discuss this issue with your lawyer before he or she closes out your case. It is almost a guarantee that this will become an issue at some point.

94. Modifying Custody

Many years ago, I was representing a client in a long, drawn out custody battle. At the end of the case, the judge indicated in the middle of his ruling that I had won. However, he concluded his ruling by saying that he was awarding temporary custody to my client. What! How is that possible I thought? Is the trial over or not? I asked the judge what happened and he indicated that custody is always temporary so this was his way of highlighting the fact.

Just like child support, custody is often modified upon a showing of changed circumstances. Unlike child support motions, these changed circumstances may not be as tangible as an increase or decrease in salary. Instead, the court will look at the best interests of the child. Thus, one judge's opinion as to the best interests of the child may be different than the judge right next door. It's one of those things that make this job fun and frustrating at the same time. Clients look to you for answers and sometimes, there are none, at least none that are solid anyway.

Sticking with a theme you have probably picked up already, the best way to win any custody application whether you are filing it or defending it is to be prepared. This goes back to meeting with your attorney and discussing all the what if scenarios.

-When should you call your lawyer about a problem?

-What happens if your ex violates the order?

-What if you want, or your ex wants to move?

-What if your child doesn't want to go with your ex?

The more prepared you are, the more likely it is that you will win the motion.

95. Talk to Your Lawyer About When to Act

No matter what motion you may be faced with, you have to know when you should act. Too many people wait to act and by then, it could be too late. My general advice to clients is to act right away but that doesn't mean they need to get me involved. Let's say their ex violates the agreement but it's not a big deal right now because it only happened once. In a calm manner, talk to your ex to find out what happened and why. See how you can ensure that it doesn't happen again.

If it is a major or repeated violation, you need to discuss a plan of attack with your lawyer. Do you rush right into court? Most of the time the answer is no. A simple letter may do the trick. If that fails, then court is probably the answer. In fact, you may have to go to court several times for the message to get through. I once had to file five motions to get my client's ex to send us the child's grade. After the third order that forced her to pay my counsel fees, I think her ex got the hint.

The worst thing you can do is nothing. This reinforces bad behavior. If you let your dog go to bathroom in your house for six months, you can't suddenly train it to then go outside. People are the same way. If your ex tests you, show them that you will not respond well to being tested. They will learn their lesson. However, you still have to abide by the lesson taught at the beginning of this book. Don't get mad. Keep your emotions out of it.

XIX. POST DIVORCE LIFE

96. Keep a Journal

As previously indicated, you should not be rushing into court over every little thing. Hopefully, you can be friends with your ex and maybe never see the inside of a court room again. I know some people like that but for every one of them, it seems like there are five more that spend most of their lives battling each other over every little thing.

Even if you are not going to rush right into court, you need to assume that you will one day be back there fighting over a number of issues. You don't want to be in a situation where you are unable to recall an event or you no longer have text messages or other evidence. So, when something happens with your ex, keep it in a journal. Your ex doesn't pick up the kids? Write it down. Your child reports that your ex's new girlfriend yelled at him today? Write it down. Be as detailed as possible. Attach all evidence for that event. Just like a diary, it should be kept in chronological order.

To put it bluntly, it really sucks that it has come down to this. I am sure that this is the last thing you want to do. However, you have to trust me that I have seen it all and I am hoping this book guides you to learn from past mistakes that others have made. You do not want to be caught years down the road without the facts and evidence you need to protect your family.

97. Save Money for Legal Fees

One of the biggest problems with our economy is that people do not save money. If everyone that called me had the ability to pay for a lawyer, I could have retired in my 30's. In fact, I often wonder how the credit card companies stay in business as it seems that there is a large percentage of people that have none at all. Thus, when there is an emergency, they have no way to hire someone to get themselves out of it.

You need a rainy day fund and I don't care how much money you make, but you need to figure out how to start one. Get a second job, change your lifestyle, shut off your cable TV, or whatever else, but start saving money now. If you don't figure out a way to save for emergencies, you are going to be in situation where you need a lawyer (or something else) and you are going to have no ability to protect yourself.

98. Don't Sweat the Small Stuff

I know, I know, this is rather cliché, but it's important. The inconsequential things people fight over because they can't follow the advice in the beginning of this book is astonishing. They act like kids fighting over every little thing. Don't be this person. Take the high road and don't stoop down to your ex's level.

If your ex does something stupid, but in the long run, it has no real impact on your life or the life of the children, don't waste your time worrying about it. You'll be much happier and richer for it. If you don't, I'll be the one richer and happier. Which would you prefer?

99. Post-Divorce Counseling

This is rare, but I am a big proponent of it. If you have children with your ex, you will be in each others lives forever. Long after the children are grown, there will be weddings, parties, funerals and holidays. Your children will want both of you there and nothing ruins a fun happy occasions like a room divided down the middle because the two of you cannot get along.

Of course, it's not always easy to bury the hatchet on your own. Thus, you should see if your ex would be interested in seeing a therapist to help you two work out some of your issues. You probably won't become best friends but if you can at least be civil towards each other, you will be happier, save money and ever more importantly, your children won't be impacted.

100. Don't Involve Children

While it's tough to get divorced without having your children impacted, you can at least get divorced without really getting them involved. Entire books are written about how to help your children deal with it and I'll let you figure out which way is best. However, I can advise you not to involve them. That is, don't talk to them about the case, don't bad mouth your ex and don't use the children as messengers. They should be 100% insulated from what is going on between the two of you.

Children are like sponges and you don't know if and when the judge will speak with them. Trust me when I tell you that you don't want to see what happens when your children tell the judge that you have been bad mouthing your ex. It's not going to be pretty. Of course, if you think your ex is doing this, call your lawyer ASAP.

101. Don't Give up the Fight

Sometimes you have to really fight for what you want. Part of fighting is dealing with all the headaches and nonsense that come with a heated divorce. I'll be honest; it's almost unbearable at times in certain cases, but if you are locked in a divorce war, you have to understand that war is ugly. You must hang in there and you must ground yourself one way or another. Read this book over and over again, especially the beginning. Find some way to take your emotions out of it and don't allow your ex or the system grind you down.

I've had clients that wanted to give in. I can think of a few that were fighting to get their children back after false allegations were made against them. Who can blame them for wanting to give up? They are spending a ton of money and they are seeing no progress. Their ex is just going to win anyway right? Well they listened to me and hung in there. Against long odds, we fought hard time after time eventually getting the allegations dismissed freeing them up to pursue custody. If they can do it so can you!